NĀLEVARNAM

OF THE FOUR COMMUNITIES OR CASTES

PAULINUS A SANCTO BARTHOLOMAEO

Edited by
JOHANN REINHOLD FORSTER

Translated by
ALEXANDER JACOB

Nālevarnam: Of the Four Communities or Castes
Paulinus a Sancto Bartholomaeo
Edited by Johann Reinhold Forster
Translated by Alexander Jacob

978-0-6486072-4-3

©Manticore Press, Melbourne, Australia, 2024.

All rights reserved, no section of this book may be utilized without permission, except brief quotations, including electronic reproductions without the permission of the copyright holders and publisher. Published in Australia.

Thema Classification: QRD (Hinduism), QRDP (Hindu Life & Practice), NH (History).

MANTICORE PRESS
WWW.MANTICORE.PRESS

CONTENTS

INTRODUCTION – *Alexander Jacob*............5

Nālevarnam

I. BRĀHMAN 33

II. KSAHTRIYA 43

III. VAISHYA 55

IV. SHŪDRA 67

INTRODUCTION

ALEXANDER JACOB

Paulinus a Sancto Bartholomaeo (1748-1806) was an Austrian Carmelite friar originally from Croatia – and called Filip Vezdin – who worked as a missionary in Kerala, in India, from 1776-1789. He returned to Rome in 1790 and became Professor of Oriental Languages at the Mission Seminary of San Pancrazio and, in 1797, Procurator for Missions. In 1798, he moved to Padua and Vienna and returned to Rome in 1800. He served as Prefect of Studies at the Urban College of Propaganda from 1803 until his death.

While in India, he learnt Malayālam and Sanskrit and produced two pioneering Sanskrit grammars, the *Sidharubam* in 1790 and the *Vyākarana* in 1804. In 1791, he published the *Systema Brahmanicum liturgicum mythologicum civile ex monumentis Indicis Musei Borgiani*, in 1794, a history of Christian missions in India *India orientalis christiana*, and, in 1796, an essay on his travels, *Viaggio alle Indie orientali*. He also wrote two works of comparative linguistics, *De antiquitate et affinitate linguae Zendicae, Samscrdamicae et Germanicae dissertatio* in 1798/99 and *De Latini sermonis origine et cum Orientalibus linguis connexione dissertatio* in 1802. His linguistic studies constitute an impressive body of Indological scholarship that paralleled the work of English Indologists like Charles Wilkins, William Jones, and Thomas Colebrooke, German ones like August Schlegel, Franz Bopp, Rudolf Roth, and Friedrich Max Müller, and French linguists like Eugène Burnouf and Abraham Anquetil-Duperron.

Paulinus' *Systema Brahmanicum liturgicum mythologicum civile* (*The Brāhmanical Liturgical, Mythological and Civil System*) was edited and translated into German in 1797 as *Darstellung der brahmanisch-indischen Götterlehre, religionsgebräuche und bürgerlichen Verfassung* (*An Account of the Brāhmanical Indian Mythology, Religious Customs, and Civil Constitution*) by the naturalist Johann Reinhold Forster (1729-1798), who also translated Paulinus' *Viaggio* in 1798 as *Reise nach Ostindien*. Paulinus' *Systema* consists of three parts: Liturgy, Mythology, and Civil Institutions. The first part contains brief descriptions of the various Brāhmanical sacrifices, and the second is a survey of the principal divinities worshipped by the Indians. The last part, entitled 'Nālevarnam,[1] or the four castes,' consists of six chapters: 'Brāhmans,' 'Kshatriyas,' 'Vaishyas,' 'Of the use of coins in India,' 'Remarks on the Indian coins in the Museum of Cardinal Borgia in Veletri,' and 'Shūdras.' In the present edition, I have translated the first, second, third, and last chapters of this work from

---

[1] Nālevarnam is the Malayālam form of the Sanskrit Chaturvarnam, four castes. Varnam is a term meaning colour and may refer to the three colours associated with the three gunas, or energetic qualities, in the Sānkhya system, sattva, rajas and tamas, represented by the colours white, red and black. The predominance of the first guna in a person denotes a brāhmanical nature, of the second a kshatriya, and of the third a vaishya/shūdra.

Forster's German translation, which excises some of the many quotations from classical authors that Paulinus includes in his work. I have also not reproduced Forster's own editorial comments on Paulinus' work.

Since the Vedas are mainly liturgical and magical incantation texts, there is not much reference to any sociological caste[2] division in the early *Rig Veda*.[3] The exceptional reference to the four castes in the Purusha Sūkta (*RV* X,90) may be explained as a later interpolation. However, even if this hymn is an interpolation, its confident ascription of the origin of the brāhmans, as well as the three other castes, to the cosmoanthropomorphic form of Purusha assumed by the divine Soul Ātman in the process of manifestation shows that the classification of society that later developed among the Indians was based initially on cosmological intuition and may have later crystallised as a socio-economic paradigm. The allotment of the four castes to the different parts of the cosmic Purusha in the Purusha Sūkta highlights the psychological differences between members of the four castes, the brāhman deriving from the mouth of the Purusha, the kshatriya his arms and the vaishya and the shūdra, the generative organs 'thighs' and the feet:

---

[2] The term 'caste' is derived from the Portuguese '*casta*', meaning a variety, class, or breed of something.

[3] John Wilson thinks 'that Caste in the ancient Vedic times was no systematic institution of the Aryas. The opinion of Dr. Max Müller, the editor of the *Rig Veda* and the most competent judge in the case, is entirely in accordance with that which we have ventured to express.' (*Indian Caste*, Edinburgh: William Blackwood and Sons, 1877, p.117).

> The Brahman was his mouth, of both his arms was the Rājanya made. His thighs became the Vaiśya, from his feet the Śūdra was produced. (*RV* X,90,12)

The primacy of the brāhman in the Purusha Sūkta is self-evident, since he represents on earth the divine Light/Brahman that forms the upper part of the Cosmic Egg or Hiranyagarbha (the lower part being Earth/Prithvi) that is the first physical manifestation of the Ātman. Besides, the division of the life of a brāhman into four stages, or āshramas, that begin with sacred study (brahmachārya) and, passing through marriage (grihastha) and renunciation (vānaprastha), culminate in metaphysical contemplation (sannyāsa) shows clearly that the entire institution of the highest of the castes is based on Yogic discipline. The composers of the Vedas themselves, the rishis, were brāhmans of the highest order and called either brahmarshis or rājarshis, showing that some kshatriyas (such as Vishvāmitra and his nephew Jamadagni) too progressed to the status of brāhmans in the course of their lives. There is indeed a close alliance between the first two castes since the duties of a kshatriya – as a ruler and soldier – are the execution of the rules established by the brāhmans.

While the kshatriya caste is primarily the king and dedicated to the maintenance of the ideal Brāhmanical order, the other castes, those of the agriculturalists/traders and artisans, are more sociological and based on professional distinctions.

Since the first three Vedas, Rig, Sāma, and Yajur, are liturgical works, it is clear that the brāhman is predominant in these. Even the *Atharva Veda* – which bears the Iranian name of Atharvan, meaning a fire-priest – extols the brāhman above the kshatriya. The *White Yajur Veda*, Adhyāya 30, however, refers to several professions along with the classical four.

In the Brāhmanas, which deal primarily with religious ritual, we find several mentions of the four castes. Thus, in the *Aitareya Brāhmana*, the three original castes are represented by the syllables akār, ukar, and makar, the initials of which constitute the sacred sound Aum. In the *Taittirīya Brāhmana*, the brāhman is associated with the gods (devas) and the shüdra with the asuras (ahuras/aesir).

In the Upanishads, which are philosophical commentaries on the Vedas, we find an interesting reference to the brāhmanical and kshatriya castes in the *Brihadāranyaka Upanishad* that probes the deep connection between these two castes and points to the brāhmanical figure as the ultimate font of creativity:

> Brahma verily was this before, one alone Being one, he did not extend, He with concentrated power created the Kshatra of elevated nature, viz, all those Kshatras who are protectors among the gods, Indra, Varuna, Soma, Rudra, Parjanya, Yama, Death and Ishana. Therefore none is greater than the Kshatra, therefore the Brahman under the Kshatriya, worships at the Rājasuya ceremony. The Kshatra alone gives (him) his glory. Brahma is thus the birth-place of the Kshatra. Therefore, although the king obtains the highest dignity, he at last takes refuge in the Brahmanas in his birth-place. Whosoever despises him, he destroys his birth-place. He is a very great sinner, like a man who mimes a superior. He did not

extend. He created the Vit (Vaishya). He is all those gods who, according to their classes, are called Vasus, Rudras, Adityas, Vishvadevas, and Maruts. He did not extend. He created the caste of the Shudras as the nourisher. This (earth) is the nourisher, for it nourishes all this whatsoever. He did not extend. He created with concentrated power Justice of eminent nature. This Justice is the preserver of the Kshatra. There is nought higher than Justice.

We note that this Upanishad's emphasis on the importance of Justice as the highest earthly virtue is quite like that of Plato in his *Republic*. However, the Upanishadic explanation of the relation between brāhmans and kshatriyas is more metaphysical than the sociological ones provided in Plato's *Republic*, Bk.II-III, of the relation between Rulers and Guardians. Further, the Platonic Rulers, who are the philosopher kings, are, in Bk.V, deemed superior for their Idealistic epistemological reasoning rather than for their genealogical excellence, as Brāhmanism generally maintains.

However, in Bk.III, 415, Plato presents a 'tale' that depicts the predominance of gold, silver, iron, and brass in the four kinds of men constituting human society, which closely resembles the Indian conception of castes:

> While all of you in the city are brothers, we will say in our tale, yet God in fashioning those of

you who are fitted to hold rule mingled gold in their generation, for which reason they are the most precious—but in the helpers silver, and iron and brass in the farmers and other craftsmen.

Though, Plato is careful to insist on the mobility of social classes:

> And as you are all akin, though for the most part you will breed after your kinds, it may sometimes happen that a golden father would beget a silver son and that a golden offspring would come from a silver sire and that the rest would in like manner be born of one another. So that the first and chief injunction that the god lays upon the rulers is that of nothing else are they to be such careful guardians and so intently observant as of the intermixture of these metals in the souls of their offspring, and if sons are born to them with an infusion of brass or iron they shall by no means give way to pity in their treatment of them, but shall assign to each the status due to his nature and thrust them out among the artizans or the farmers. And again, if from these there is born a son with unexpected gold or silver in his composition they shall honour such and bid them go up higher, some to the office of guardian, some to the assistanceship, alleging that there is an oracle that the state shall then be overthrown when the man of iron or brass is its guardian.

We note, further, that Plato's discussion, in Bk.IV, 439-41, of the tripartite division of the soul bears some resemblance to the psychological basis of caste division mentioned in the *Gītā*, Ch.18,41-45, following the Sāṅkhya conception of sattva, rajas, and tamas as characterising the brāhmanical, kshatriya and vaishya/shūdra respectively. However, rather than classifying men into three or four types, Plato merely insists that the rational aspect of the soul along with its auxiliary, the spirited aspect, must rule over the lowest animal aspect of it (Bk.IV,441).

The division of labour in societies itself is, in Plato (Bk.II, 369ff), attributable to the lower economic demands of human beings. The higher, civilisatory, aspects of society derive from a desire for luxurious refinements of fundamental physical pleasures (373ff). The passions indulged in by this second, luxurious, aspect of society necessitate wars and the regular maintenance of the state. These must be conducted by 'auxiliaries' – the warriors – as well as by the administrators of justice, such as the police force and the government (with its judicial, legislative, and executive powers). The latter will act as the 'guardians' of the state. The real 'rulers' of the state, however, are the philosophers (with deliberative powers), who are characterised by the knowledge of good and evil (Bk.X, 611-613).

We see that the Platonic auxiliaries and guardians are more closely allied to the last than to the first inasmuch as they execute the rules established by the philosophers. While the philosophers represent wisdom, the guardians and auxiliaries maintain honour, and the rest of the population are driven by material gain or advantage. This close association of the first two classes of the Platonic republic is similar to that which we have noticed also in the Vedas.

However, in Diodorus Siculus' 1st century B.C. account of the caste divisions in ancient Athens, the author refers to an Egyptian origin of both the Athenian city and its society:

> Even the Athenians, they say, are colonists from Saïs in Egypt, and they undertake to offer proofs of such a relationship; for the Athenians are the only Greeks who call their city "Asty," a name brought over from the city Asty in Egypt. Furthermore, their body politic had the same classification and division of the people as found in Egypt, where the citizens have been divided into three orders: the first Athenian class consisted of the "eupatrids," as they were called, being those who were such as had received the best education and were held worthy of the highest honour, as is the case with the priests of Egypt; the second was that of the "geomoroi," who were expected to possess arms and to serve in defence of the state, like those in Egypt who are known as husbandmen and supply the warriors; and the last class was reckoned to be that of the "demiurgoi," who practise the mechanical arts and render only the most menial services to the state, this class among the Egyptians having a similar function.[4]

We see that there were originally three castes both in Egypt and in Athens and that the warriors were derived

---

[4] Diodorus Siculus, *Bibliotheca Historica*, Bk.I, Ch.28.

from the 'husbandmen' or vaishyas. The priests and the king constituted the highest section of Egyptian society, while the warriors were, like the priests, formed into a hereditary caste endowed with landed property;

> For it would be absurd to entrust the safety of the entire nation to these men and yet have them possess in the country no property to fight for valuable enough to arouse their ardour. But the most important consideration is the fact that, if they are well-to do, they will readily beget children and thus so increase the population that the country will not need to call in any mercenary troops. And since their calling, like that of the priests, is hereditary, the warriors are incited to bravery by the distinguished records of their fathers and, inasmuch as they become zealous students of warfare from their boyhood up, they turn out to be invincible by reason of their daring and skill.[5]

The husbandmen (along with herdsmen) and craftsmen who constituted the remainder of Egyptian society did not own land and pursued their respective occupations without any social mobility. Indeed, according to Diodorus, 'among the Egyptians if any artisan should take part in public affairs or pursue several crafts he is severely punished.'[6]

The question of the Egyptian, that is, Hamitic and pre-Āryan, origin of Athenian culture is complicated by Diodorus' assertion that the 'Dionysus' who – according to Megasthenes and Arrian, cited by

---

[5] *Ibid.*, Bk.I, Ch.73.

[6] *Ibid.*, Bk.I, Ch.74.

Paulinus[7] – brought agriculture and the arts to India was in fact 'Osiris', who marched

> through Arabia along the shore of the Red Sea as far as India and the limits of the inhabited world. He also founded not a few cities in India, one of which he named Nysa, wishing to leave there a memorial of that city in Egypt where he had been reared. He also planted ivy in the Indian Nysa, and throughout India and those countries which border upon it the plant to this day is still to be found only in this region. And many other signs of his stay he left in that country, which have led the Indians of a later time to lay claim to the god and say that he was by birth a native of India.[8]

In the Indian Sūtras, especially the *Shrautasūtra* of Kātyāyana, the caste distinctions become more rigid and neither the kshatriyas nor the vaishyas are permitted to maintain the sacred Gārhapatya fire, while the shūdras are excluded from the wearing of the sacred thread and the conduct of sacrifices. In general, in the Sūtras, the shūdras have a servile social position. On the other hand, it may be noted that, in the *Mānavakalpa Sūtra*, brāhmans 'who take care of cattle, who trade, who practise mechanical and sportive arts, who are usurers, are to be treated as shūdras.'

In the *Mahābhārata*, Vana Parva, too, we note – in the conversation between Yudhishtira and the serpent – a similar insistence on the identification of caste with character:

---

[7] See below p.55n.
[8] *Ibid.*, Bk.I, Ch.19

> The Serpent replies: The establishment of the four castes is with proof (authorized) and Brahma is also true. But even in Shūdras, O Yudishthira, are truth, liberality, wrathlessness, innocence, abstinence from killing, compassion. Knowledge (of Brahma) is also without pain or pleasure, O Lord of men, and without these (sensations) there is no other thing but Knowledge. Yudhishtira says: When in a Shūdra there is a mark of virtue, and it is not in a Dvija (twice-born), the Shūdra is not a Shūdra and the Brāhman is not a Brāhman. The person in whom that mark of virtue is seen, O Serpent, is a Brāhman, and the person in whom it is not seen is a Shūdra.[9]

In the law book, *Manusmrithi*, which is mostly a textbook of the duties of the brāhmans and the kshatriyas (again studied mostly as a royal, rather than a soldierly, caste), the Vedic derivation of the castes from the Purusha is repeated:

> Ch.I, 87. But in order to protect this universe He, the most resplendent one, assigned separate (duties and) occupations to those who sprang from his mouth, arms, thighs, and feet.
>
> 88. To Brahmanas he assigned teaching and studying (the Veda), sacrificing for their own benefit and for others, giving and accepting (of alms).

---

[9] Quoted in Wilson, *op.cit.*, p.254.

89. The Kshatriya he commanded to protect the people, to bestow gifts, to offer sacrifices, to study (the Veda), and to abstain from attaching himself to sensual pleasures;

90. The Vaisya to tend cattle, to bestow gifts, to offer sacrifices, to study (the Veda), to trade, to lend money, and to cultivate land.

91. One occupation only the lord prescribed to the Shudra, to serve meekly even these (other) three castes.

The sharp distinctions of the castes are presented again in Ch.VIII:

410. (The king) should order a Vaisya to trade, to lend money, to cultivate the land, or to tend cattle, and a Sudra to serve the twice-born castes.

411. (Some wealthy) Brahmana shall compassionately support both a Kshatriya and a Vaisya, if they are distressed for a livelihood, employing them on work (which is suitable for) their (castes).

…

413. But a Shudra, whether bought or unbought, he may compel to do servile work; for he was created by the Self-existent (Svayambhu) to be the slave of a Brahmana.

414. A Shudra, though emancipated by his master, is not released from servitude; since

> that is innate in him, who can set him free from it?

and in Ch.X:

> 4. Brahmana, the Kshatriya, and the Vaisya castes (varna) are the twice-born ones, but the fourth, the Shudra, has one birth only; there is no fifth (caste).

Manu elaborates on the spiritual excellence of the brāhmans in Ch.I:

> 92. Man is stated to be purer above the navel (than below); hence the Self-existent (Svayambhu/Purusha) has declared the purest (part) of him (to be) his mouth.
>
> 93. As the Brahmana sprang from (Brahman's) mouth, as he was the first-born, and as he possesses the Veda, he is by right the lord of this whole creation.
>
> 94. For the Self-existent (Svayambhu), having performed austerities, produced him first from his own mouth, in order that the offerings might be conveyed to the gods and manes and that this universe might be preserved.
>
> 95. What created being can surpass him, through whose mouth the gods continually consume the sacrificial viands and the manes the offerings to the dead?

as well as on their social eminence:

96. Of created beings the most excellent are said to be those which are animated; of the animated, those which subsist by intelligence; of the intelligent, mankind; and of men, the Brahmanas;

97. Of Brahmanas, those learned (in the Veda); of the learned, those who recognise (the necessity and the manner of performing the prescribed duties); of those who possess this knowledge, those who perform them; of the performers, those who know the Brahman.

98. The very birth of a Brahmana is an eternal incarnation of the sacred law; for he is born to (fulfil) the sacred law, and becomes one with Brahman.

99. A Brahmana, coming into existence, is born as the highest on earth, the lord of all created beings, for the protection of the treasury of the law.

The excellence of the kshatriyas is declared in Ch.VII, where we note again the particular superiority of their physical and psychological constitution:

> 2. A Kshatriya, who has received according to the rule the sacrament prescribed by the Veda, must duly protect this whole (world).
>
> 3. For, when these creatures, being without a king, through fear dispersed in all directions, the Lord created a king for the protection of this whole (creation),

> 4. Taking (for that purpose) eternal particles of Indra, of the Wind, of Yama, of the Sun, of Fire, of Varuna, of the Moon, and of the Lord of wealth (Kubera).
>
> 5. Because a king has been formed of particles of those lords of the gods, he therefore surpasses all created beings in lustre;
>
> 6. And, like the sun, he burns eyes and hearts; nor can anybody on earth even gaze on him.
>
> 7. Through his (supernatural) power he is Fire and Wind, he Sun and Moon, he the Lord of justice (Yama), he Kubera, he Varuna, he great Indra.

The king must first and foremost maintain the divinely, or cosmically, instituted castes in his society:

> 35. The king has been created (to be) the protector of the castes (varna) and orders, who, all according to their rank, discharge their several duties.

The chief political duty of the kshatriya is the protection of his subjects:

> 144. The highest duty of a Kshatriya is to protect his subjects, for the king who enjoys the rewards, just mentioned, is bound to (discharge that) duty.

The vaishya's duties are, in the *Mārkandeya Purāna*, defined thus: 'trade, cattle-tending and agriculture are his means of livelihood', while the shūdra is, in the *Arthashāstra,* associated with arts and crafts.

However, in general, compared to the spiritual eminence of the brāhman, the shūdra occupies a lowly status. Since the shūdra is born of the feet of the cosmic Purusha, he cannot become 'dvija' or twice-born and cannot conduct sacrifices. He can only aspire to the status of a brāhman in another life by serving brāhmans in this.

The term 'shūdra' may initially have belonged to a non-Āryan tribe dwelling in the region of Συδρος on the lower Indus[10] that the Āryans, originally comprised of three castes, must have subjugated and recruited as cultivators and artisans. It is not known if the Συδρος region may be related to the pastoral tribe that still speaks Brahui, a Dravidian language, in Pakistan.

Whether the Brāhmanical religion was originally Egyptian-Hamitic[11] or Āryan-Japhetic, it is clear that Brāhmanism as formulated by the Indo-Āryans was an exclusively fire-worshipping cult. For the Āryans designated the Dasyus or non-Āryans as Anagni, the

---

[10] See Ptolemy, *Geographia,* VI,20,3; VII, I, 61. The brāhmans themselves are located by Ptolemy south of the Bettigus mountain (VII,1), which may have formed part of the Pamir mountains in north-eastern Afghanistan, and the Parsis in the Paropamisades (VI, 18), which is north of Arachosia and identical to Gandhāra, its Old Persian name. Thus, the Indians and Iranians were probably resident in the same region, or neighbouring ones, originally.

[11] F.E. Pargiter, for instance, had maintained that Brāhmanism itself was not originally Āryan but adopted into Indo-Āryan religion from Dravidian (see F.E. Pargiter, *Ancient Indian Historical Tradition,* London: Milford, 1922, Ch.26).

fireless and the reference in Manusmrithi X:43-45 to "the Dravidas, the Kāmbojas, the Yavanas [Ionians], the Sakas [Scythians], etc." as kshatriya races which have sunk to the level of shūdras on account of their neglect of the sacred rites and the authority of the brāhmans suggests that Brāhmanism was conserved more carefully by the Indo-Āryans than by any other ethnic group.

The Āryans themselves derive their name from the land that they originally inhabited called Airyanem Vaejah, which has been – uncertainly – identified by some scholars with the region around Khwarazm,[12] whose name reflects the term Xvarenah, or glory, that depicts the golden light of Ouranos/Dyaus. The Indian Āryans, like the Iranians, name themselves, and their settlement in India, Āryāvarta, after this original homeland of the Āryans.

In the *Bhavishya Purāna*, there is, as noted by Professor H.H. Wilson and John Wilson, reference to the 'Magas,' silent worshippers of the sun, from Shakadvipa, one of the seven galaxies or 'continents' of the primal lotus formation of Earth.[13] The term Maga

---

[12] Khwarazm is today shared by Uzbekistan and Turkmenistan.

[13] In the Purānas (*Padma Purāna* I,39,153-4), the Cosmic Egg or Hiranyagarbha is said to be constituted of a lotus formation of Earth surmounted by the heavenly light of Brahman. Earth contains seven "dvīpas" or islands (called continents in the Avestan literature) that are formed due to the whirling action of the first manifestation of the Divine Light called Priyavrata (*Bhāgavata Purāna*, V,1,30-32) (This cosmic event is reflected in the Hieronyman Orphic fragment (78), where Protogonos wheels round the world in his chariot to bring light to it; see M.L. West, *The Orphic Poems*, Oxford: Clarendon Press, 1983, p.214).

The seven islands are named Jambudwīpa, Plakshadwīpa, Shakadwīpa, halmalidswīpa, Kushadwīpa, Krounchadwīpa and Pushkaradwīpa and may refer to continents that are arranged

prompts an identification with the Iranian Magis. While the brāhmans in the land of the Shakas are called Magas, the kshatriyas are called Magasas, the vaishyas Manasas, and the shūdras Mandagas.[14] This again suggests the unity of the Indo-Iranian tribes before their separation into Asura-worshipping and Deva-worshipping groups.

The frequent Indic references to the Asuras as the enemies of the Devās, however, indicates that the Indian Āryans had separated from the Iranian at the time of the composition of the Vedas, for the Iranians – as well as the followers of the Odinic religion that spread from the region round the Don River in Russia through Anatolia to the Balkans and Europe[15] – venerate their highest deities as 'Ahura' and 'Aesir' respectively.

The references to the Sindhu (Indus) river in the *Rig Veda* suggest that the early Vedas were composed near this river. The most probable location of the development of the original Brāhmanical religion is in Gandhāra region (north-west Pakistan/north-east Afghanistan) in Bactria, not far from the Indus. Evidence of fire-altars such as those used in Brāhmanical sacrifices is found in the Bactro-Margiana Archaeological Complex from the third millennium B.C. We have noted that the Āryans designated the Dasyus or non-Āryans as Anagni, the fireless. The reference in *Manusmrithi* X:43-45 to "the Dravidas, the Kāmbojas, the Yavanas [Ionians], the

---

concentrically around the innermost, Jambudwīpa. At the centre of Jambudwīpa rises the golden mountain Meru. Jambudwīpa itself is divided into nine regions, Bhārata, Indra, Ksheruman, Tāmravarna, Gabhistaman, Nāga, Saumya, Gandharva and Varuna. Bhārata is the name given to the modern Indian state.

[14] See Wilson, *op.cit.*, p.438.

[15] See Snorri Sturluson, *Prose Edda*, 'Prologue', and *Heimskringla* ('Ynglingasaga').

Sakas [Scythians], etc." as kshatriya races which have sunk to the level of shūdras on account of their neglect of the sacred rites and the authority of the brāhmans suggests that Brāhmanism was formulated by the Indo-Āryans as an exclusive fire-worshipping cult.

The BMAC is not far north of Mundigak, where from 3000 B.C. we notice extensions of Elamite culture resembling that of the Indus Valley.[16] It is difficult to determine whether the Āryan settlements of BMAC represent a continuation of the early Elamite Hurrians of Mundigak or are new immigrants from the Andronovo culture associated with the Indo-Āryans (1800-900 B.C.).[17] The latter is indeed the more probable. The Andronovo culture is itself derived from the Hut Grave and Catacomb Grave culture of 2800-2000 B.C.[18] and the Sintashta culture of the southeast Urals (2300-1900 B.C.),[19] which is marked by chariot burials and may have been proto-Āryan rather than proto-Indo-Āryan. The fact that there is clear evidence

---

[16] Herodotus's description of the inhabitants of the various satrapies of Darius suggests that this region in Afghanistan may have been settled by Bactrians (Darius' 12th province) or Sattagydae, Gandaridae, Dadicae and Aparytae (7th province) (cf. J.P. Mallory and V.H. Mair, *The Tarim Mummies: Ancient China and the mystery of the earliest peoples from the West*, London: Thames and Hudson, 2008, p.45f.; p.262).

[17] Andronovo type pottery has been found in the early layers of Margiana (see A. Parpola, "The problem of the Aryans," G. Erdosy, (ed.) *The Indo-Aryans of Ancient South Asia*, Berlin: Walter de Gruyter, 1995, p.363).

[18] The Hut Grave culture apparently separated into the Timber Grave (proto-Iranian) and Andronovo (proto-Āryan) cultures. The fourth millennium predecessor of the Hut Grave and Catacomb Grave cultures may have been the Yamnaya culture dating from 3500-2800 B.C. (*ibid.*, p.356).

[19] See J.P. Mallory and V.H. Mair, *op. cit.*, pp.260f.

of fire-worship in the BMAC and little evidence of it in Mundigak suggests that the former is derived from the Andronovo rather than from the Elamite colonies.

The elaborate fire altars evident in the ruins of the BMAC complex attest to the performance of the Āryan fire-sacrifices. The temples also contain rooms with "all the necessary apparatus for the preparation of drinks extracted from poppy, hemp and ephedra" that may have been used for the soma-rituals.[20] It is interesting to note too, in this context, that the Avesta (which is geographically centred in eastern Iran) mentions the Māzanian daevas as worshippers of the Indian gods. According to Burrow, Māzana is known in Iranian sources as the territory between the southern shore of the Caspian Sea and the Alburz mountains.[21] It may be related also to Margiana and the Indo-Āryan culture noted there.

When we turn to the 4th c. B.C. Greek accounts of India, we find in the *Indica* (fragment XXXIII=Strabo XV) of Megasthenes, the Greek ambassador of Seleucus Nicator at the court of Chandragupta Maurya, that he divides the population of India into seven groups, the first being that of the philosophers (that is, the brāhmans), the second farmers, the third shepherds (these two groups corresponding to the vaishya), the fourth artisans (corresponding to the shūdra), the fifth

---

[20] *Ibid*, p.262.

[21] See E. Bryant, *The Quest for the Origins of Vedic Culture: the Indo-Aryan Migration Debate*, Oxford: Oxford University Press, 2001, p.130.

the military (corresponding to the kshatriya), the sixth the overseers and superintendents of the country, and the seventh constituted of councillors, or advisors to the king, judges, and army generals.

Megasthenes (fragment XLI=Strabo, XV, i) further divides the Indian philosophers into Brāhmans and Sarmans, the former spending the first thirty-seven years of their life as students of philosophy, brahmachārya, and the rest of their lives as grhasta (householders). The Sarmans are divided into the 'Hylobioi,' who live as hermits in the forest (rather like the followers of the vānaprastha stage/āshrama of Vedic life), the physicians (practicing something like Āyurveda), and lastly mendicant diviners and magicians. The Sarmana or Shramana tradition may have been an ascetic branch of ancient Brāhmanical religion that was later adopted by Jains and Buddhists (hence the later identification of this sect by its Pāli name). Paulinus too mentions brāhmans and samanaens (from samana, the Pali form of Sanskrit shramana) as two different sorts of religious traditions.

In the late eighteenth century, the early British historians of the East India Company, such as Colin Mackenzie (1754-1821) and Mark Wilks (1759-1831),[22] did not refer much to castes.[23] Nineteenth century studies

---

[22] Mark Wilks wrote a work called *Historical Sketches of the South of India, in an attempt to trace the history of Mysoor*, 3 vols., London, 1810.

[23] See Nicholas Dirks, *Castes of Mind: Colonialism and the Making of New India*, Princeton, NJ: Princeton University Press, 2001, pp.28ff.

like the Englishman John Wilson's *Indian Caste* (2 volumes, 1877), however, were quite elaborate and more informative than Paulinus' account of the Indian castes. Nevertheless, in the latter work, we have some of the earliest first-hand observations of how the caste system operated in India, especially in South India – where the Hindu tradition was better preserved than in the north –, at the end of the eighteenth and the beginning of the nineteenth century.

As regards the origin of the caste system itself, Paulinus rightly traces it back to Manu:

> there is however a firm and general tradition among the Brāhmans, that is, that the civil constitution and political institution of India springs not from the sun, the moon or the planets but from King Manu, the founder of the Indian nation, whom Vishnu freed, on account of his good works, from the devastation of the Flood.

He divides the brāhmans into six sects, the Vaishnavite, Shaivite, Smārta, the Atheistic, the Shaktiist, and the Sarvagnya (who do not adhere to any particular sect) and describes their characteristic socio-religious customs.

The kshatriyas are described as being both rulers and soldiers and the several duties of this caste are detailed. Paulinus further enumerates the different divisions of an Indian army. He remarks that the kshatriya caste has not been preserved as an exclusive one since shūdras and Nairs (a major, originally matrilineal, community of Malabār) have been enlisted in the military service. He describes, in particular, the matriarchal society of the Nairs, which may have followed customs prevalent among the kshatriyas and contributed to the military strength of this caste, since the woman is in charge of the family and the man does not have to concern himself much with its maintenance.

As regards the vaishyas, Paulinus notes:

> As respected and revered as the first and second caste are in India so much too is this third since it stands in closest relationship with them and is utterly indispensable and does not practise any dishonest business and constitutes the foundation of the entire state. Here there does not enter at all any thought of trade that promotes luxury among these and weakens the strength of the empire but the legislation is characterized even here by its simplicity in that it restricts the lifestyle, work and occupation of this third noble caste to farming, animal husbandry and to trade with the products gained from these.

Paulinus proceeds to describe the methods of farming employed by the vaishya Indians. He believes that the varied seasonal requirements of farming encouraged the development of astronomy too among the brāhmans. and 'that this science, along with its astronomical fables and eastern allegories, was transferred from them to Greece and Latium.'

Unlike in Manu's law book, the shūdras of India as observed by Paulinus constitute a 'noble' caste constituted of

> the artists and handicraftsmen which contributes no less than the other three to the maintenance of the kingdom and was, therefore, at the time this political institution was created, honoured with nobility. To this caste belong goldsmiths, metal casters, smiths, carpenters, garland makers, painters, doctors, tailors, fortune-tellers, magicians, cloth weavers, and many other workers.

But this classification, as G.S. Ghurye pointed out, is not found in the *Rig Veda*:

> Besides the four orders are mentioned in the Rigveda occupations like blacksmith, leather-worker, barber, physician, goldsmith, merchant and chariot-builder. We do not know which of these occupations were comprised in any of the four orders, nor can we say that each of them constituted a separate class.[24]

The only two non-noble groups are the pariahs and the puleyas, the former being considered outcasts because their profession as tanners forced them to work with the corpses of animals and the latter constituted of those who had transgressed against their caste regulations and were therefore reduced to a condition of slavery.

We see that, already in the eighteenth century, the rigorous caste distinctions insisted on by Manu have been diluted, no doubt because of the fact that, while the religious nature of the lives of the brāhmans

---

[24] G.S. Ghurye, *Caste and Race in India*, London: Routledge and Kegan Paul, 1932, p.51.

preserved this caste in a relatively intact form, the more professionally orientated kshatriya caste tended, for practical military reasons, to admit intermixtures from the vaishya and shūdra castes, which came to be considered 'noble' (*nobilis*) as a result.

Paulinus also points to the institution of guild-like associations among the shūdras headed by kulashreshtas, who served as the judges of the guilds. Even the role of these kulashreshtas began to be reduced when the kshatriyas, who were already rather mixed, sought to dominate their judicial office.

As regards the sculptors and artists of India, Paulinus notes that, while Indian sculpture lacks the elegance of the Graeco-Romans, it nevertheless represents the qualities of the gods depicted in a more accurate symbolical manner. As doctors, Indians do not focus on surgery on account of their aversion to any process involving blood-letting, though they have developed a great mastery of herbal medicine. Finally, Paulinus mentions the scribes and their production, throughout Indian history, of numerous documents written first on palm leaves and later, with the invention of paper, on sheets of paper. Copper plates too were then used for the inscription of official notifications such as laws, privileges, and land-grants.

NĀLEVARNAM

OF THE FOUR COMMUNITIES OR CASTES

BRĀHMAN

As the Indians derived most of the main principles of their religion from astronomy, many of their civil institutions also seem to be derived from the same or a similar source. All of antiquity was of the opinion that certain divine intelligences animated the sun, the moon, the planets and the other stars and to that is also related the derivation, among the Indians, of their kings from the sun and the moon, who fall accordingly into two classes, of which the first – as I have partially shown elsewhere – is called Sūryavamsham and the other Somavamsham. The former includes the kings that derive from the sun, the latter the kings who derive from the moon. This is confirmed also by the narration of many Greek writers who, along with the vulgar opinion of the Indians, attribute to Bacchus the rise of the Indian empire and its civic institution. But Bacchus is, as was already demonstrated above, Shiva, the sun.

Arrian narrates that Bacchus left behind to the Indians his son Budya, as his successor in the empire. But Budya is none but that astronomical divinity Buddha, Dharma, or Mercury, to whom the Indians, Tibetans, and Egyptians attribute instruction in laws and the sciences. Shri Rāma also is supposed, according to similar statements of Greek and Indian writers, to have brought India under his dominion and controlled this country, and introduced not only farming and laws but also cultivated the people through its civil constitution. But Shri Rāma was born, as we already know, from the star Rohini.[25]

TAB XXVIII – *(a) Brāhman – after an Indian painting in the Museo Borgiano*
(b) The wife of a brāhman – after a painting in the Museo Borgiano

Even the philosophical institutes of the Samanaens[26] stand in closest relationship to astronomy in that

---

[25] [Rohini is the consort of Chandra, the moon god. Rāma is also called Rāmachandra.] [N.B. All notes in brackets are by the translator.]

[26] [Samanaeans refers to the Samanas, the Pali form of Sanskrit Shramanas, or ascetics. Of them the hermits are considered the most austere. Paulinus' depiction of them as bearing marks of the lingam on their bodies suggests that they may have been a Hindu sect rather than a Buddhist. This sect, as well as others, is noted in several Greek historians such as Megasthenes, *Indica*, frag.LXI, Arrian, *Indica* XV,i, Strabo, *Geographia*, Bk.XV, Clement of Alexandria, *Stromata*, Bk.I, Ch.15, Porphyry, *De abstinentia*, Bk.IV, 17-18.]

these people maintain that they worship the highest Being through the symbols of the sun, the moon, and the planets, that the lingam[27] that they bear on their neck or arms is a symbol of the creative sun and that they finally worship in public religious services the creative, sustaining and destructive power of the sun through the symbols of the earth, water, and fire. These Samanaeans, hesychasts,[28] 'munis,' or contemplative people are generally the advisors of the kings because, in the astronomical world, even the sun and the moon appear as kings that the other planets as it were serve.

Now, in this relation of earthly matters to the astronomical observation of the universe is the basis of the religious and civil establishment and constitution of India, as this is illustrated also by the great number of kings, philosophers, cities, tribes, and other individual persons who have received their names from the sun and the moon and are even now named after the stars.[29] Now from this arose, perhaps, that confusion of things and persons in ancient history, for indeed many things

---

[27] [The divine phallus representing the universe and the sun that arises out of it.]

[28] [Hesychasts is the term for the contemplative monks of the Eastern Christian Orthodox tradition.]

[29] Even today the names Mitra, Mahādeva, Krishna, Rāma, etc. very common masculine names and likewise the women also are often called Kāli, Pārvathi, Shakti, Īshvari, etc. Those names of men are, as is evidenced from what has been said before, derived from the sun and the stars, those of women from the moon. Indeed some of the latter, for example, Lakshmi, Shree, Ramā, Umā, etc. refer to the Earth, or the rulers in it. Similarly even the names of kings, cities and temples derived from the sun or the moon as, for example, Chandrakot, the lunar city, Rājyamitra, King Mitra or the sun (wrongly Rājamirda), Rājarama (wrongly Rājarāna on De L'Isle's map), Rāmeshvaram, the temple of Lord Rāma, Rāmapuram, the city of Rāma, Krishnapuram, etc.

or persons were designated in one and the same place, or city, with one and the same name since everything was differentiated only by its class name, and the art of writing was still lacking. In this great confusion there is, however, a firm and general tradition among the Brāhmans, that is, that the civil constitution and political institution of India springs not from the sun, the moon, or the planets but from King Manu, the founder of the Indian nation, whom Vishnu freed, on account of his good works, from the devastation of the Flood.[30]

Manu thus gave to the Indians its national system derived from astronomy and divided its inhabitants into four classes, namely, priests, kings, farmers, and craftsmen.[31] These four classes, which bear the names Brāhman, Kshatriya, Vaishya, and Shūdra, are the principal castes of the Indians but contain, according to the condition of civil occupations, many sub-divisions, whose number runs to eighty eight. As regards those principal castes, meanwhile, each of them has its

---

[30] This flood appears under different names. Thus it is called Pralayam, a universal devastation, Vellapralayam, the universal devastation through water, Kalpānda, the end of stability, justice, morality, Kshaeya, total annihilation, Samvarta, universal disintegration or the destruction of all earthly things. This flood was the work of evil spirits and their intention of destroying the world would have succeeded if Vishnu, on the request of the good spirits, had not appeared in the form of a fish, and later of a tortoise, and saved from the universal destruction King Manu and eight persons who raised up the world that was close to sinking. Vishnu himself narrated when he appeared in the form of Krishna, that his ancestors, the Kauravās were saved from the flood and that he assumed the form of one of them in order to fight for the Pāndavas. Thereafter the Indians begin their history with Manu, set the epoch of their silver age in this flood, and derive from that time their laws and institutions.

[31] [This classification according to Manu is more scholarly than the seven-fold division of Indians to be found in Megasthenes, and in Arrian following him.]

characteristic laws, customs, and practices; those who belong to one cannot move into or be resituated in another; they may not also marry one into another caste but must remain loyal to their caste and their occupations. Nevertheless, there are cases in which they all agree with one another. One of these is the acknowledgement of the highest Being whom they worship through the symbol of the sun, fire, and water, the expectation of the reward of virtue and punishment of crime or, in other words, the expectation of fame through Shiva or Vishnu and the fear of Shiva as the Judge of the Dead and the Lord of the Underworld, and further the belief in the transmigration of souls from one body into another, the reverence of the cow, obedience towards kings, the reverence of Brāhmans, the special respect for teachers, the washing of the body, atonement through prayers and fasts, the fear of evil spirits, helpful outreach to the poor of the same caste, the acceptance and accommodation of such strangers, the demonstration of courtesy towards the same and, finally, the abstention from the courtesans of another caste.

The Brāhmans are, as regards people and land, different to the Brāhmans in Nepal who live closest to Tibet, the Gauri or the Bengalis who live by the Ganges, the Sindhis who are falsely called Hindus and live by the Indus, the Telugus, Mogolitans or the Brāhmans around Agram, the Marāthis, Karnatakas, Kanarese, Tamils, Malabāris, Mysoreans, and those of Madurai. But with regard to their official functions all these are either sacrificial priests or religious teachers; they are either Grahastas, that is, married, or Grahashāstris, that is, astronomers, or Jyotishashāstris, as the astrologers among them are called.

With regard to the division among the Brāhmans based on certain principles of belief, many sects of the same are to be noted. The first of these sects is that of the Vaishnavites who are called Vishnubhaktis and worship the god Vishnu, or the principle of water, in a very special way. These are divided further into two schools. One of them is that of the Tattvavādis – or Mādhava Vaishnavites, who maintain that they ceaselessly worship the truth or the true and highest Being through the symbol of Vishnu. For this reason, they are also called 'Those who love the Truth,' for tattvam means truth,[32] and a true Being that exists of its own accord. Their name of Mādhavās is taken from the founder[33] of this school.

The second sect of Vaishnavites is called Rāmānujas, after its founder Rāmānuja.[34] The followers of the same consider Vishnu as a hermaphrodite and therefore attribute to him a male as well as a female gender, but also an active and a passive force. They believe in rewards and punishments after death, live unmarried, and follow one teacher. They are generally differentiated from the followers of other sects and schools by certain marks painted on the forehead and chest, of which the female yoni, in yellow or red, as a symbol of fire and water, or of warmth and moisture, is the most common.

The second sect is that of the Shaivites or Shiva Bhaktis who worship Shiva, that is, the sun or fire. To this god they ascribe the creation of the universe,

---

[32] [Tattva means, literally, 'reality'.]

[33] [Mādhava (ca.1200-ca.1300) was a major Vaishnav philosopher of Karnātaka, in South India, who founded the Dvaita (dualist) school of Vedāntic (Upanishadic) philosophy.]

[34] [Rāmānuja (ca.1077-1157) was a Vaishnav philosopher of Tamilnād, who propounded a Vishishtadvaita (qualified non-dualist) form of Vedāntic philosophy.]

consider him as the cause and the principle of all things, attribute to him the creative, sustaining, and destructive power, and indeed do not reject Vishnu or water but find his powers all united in Shiva or the sun. Symbols of the worship of this sect are cones, obelisks, lingams, yonis, and triangles. The horns of the moon, the disc of the sun, Shiva's eye rising from the middle of his forehead, the pentagram, the lingam, and other similar marks that they consider sacred and divine they bear depicted on the forehead and chest. The lotus flower, seashell, and the double triangle, or pentagram, are also the insignia of the King of Travancore, which he bears in his flags and rings.

The third Brāhmanical sect is called Smārta[35] and this word means a man who contemplates unceasingly and seriously, and is fully sunk in thought. Shankara guru[36] is called the founder of this sect and those who belong to it maintain that Vishnu and Shiva are not different but one and the same god. At the same time they ascribe the creative and destructive force to a single being and consider them as indivisible and closely bound to each other. This sect, therefore, clearly proves that the investigations of the Indian wisemen through the symbols of water and fire were related to something else, that is, to the creative, sustaining, and destructive force, the attribute of the true god that is found in a single, that is, in the highest, Being and is, in relation to the efficient cause, indivisible, but in God alone can be noticed and differentiated through the understanding and deliberation. If the investigations of the Brāhmans

---

[35] [The term 'smārta' means, literally, that which is derived from Smriti, or a specific literary religious tradition, as distinct from Shruti, the revealed scriptures, such as the Vedas.]

[36] [Shankara (8th c.) was a Kerala brāhman who developed the Advaita (non-dualist) school of Vedāntic philosophy.]

were related only to the symbol of water and fire, or the creative and destructive force of the sun, how would they be able to consider fire and water as one and the same thing but the creative, sustaining, and destructive force as indivisible? That they differed much here from one another and divided themselves into sects was perhaps to be expected given such speculative investigations.

That which has just been mentioned is confirmed sufficiently by the fourth Brāhmanical sect. It includes in itself the Pāshāndists, who believe in nothing, deny the attributes of god, acknowledge no god, and stand in opposition to the other sects. Pāshānda means one who denies god, a man to whom divinity is abhorrent, resists it, and so it is now illuminating that these people acknowledged a highest Being, pondered over the divine characteristics under those symbols and were finally divided – according to their imperfect idea of this Being, and of their varied interpretation and divisions of it, and their ignorance of the manner in which these characteristics are found in the divinity – into diverse sects that still exist now. According to this, earth, water, fire, or the sun are nothing but symbols through which the creative, sustaining, and destructive power of God is apprehended and is in this way worshipped by the Brāhmans. Īshvara is the Lord, or the highest Being, but Shakti his power, or imagined wife, through which he operates. Of the former the sun is the symbol, of the latter the moon. Brahman or the earth designates further the creative characteristic of this highest Being, Vishnu or water the sustaining, and Shiva or fire the destructive characteristic.

The fifth sect of the Brāhmans consists of the Shaktīsts, or Parāshaktīsts, and bears the name of Shaktībhaktīsts. They maintain that the goddess Shakti is Nature or that efficient force through which god has created everything, she is the highest Being, and the creative cause of the earth, water, and fire, or of Brahman, Vishnu, and Shiva, indeed, finally, the wife and mother of these gods. That they have obtained their name from this goddess does not perhaps need to be remarked. But as symbols and marks of the Shakti she is served by the triangle, the yoni, the lotus, and the moon. Furthermore, this sect forms from the goddess whom they worship a second figure, namely that of a creator and destroyer, as was shown in greater detail earlier when we treated of Bhavāni.[37]

The sixth or last sect of Brāhmans bears the name Sarvagnya. Their members maintain that they know everything but do not wish to belong to any of the mentioned sects. They believe in a highest divine Being, but the world is, in their opinion, directed only by chance and without any special providence and exists through the power provided to it at one time.

The Grahasta Brāhmans enter into a real and indivisible marriage with a single woman; but if the latter is not fruitful they repudiate her in the presence of a judge and their guru or teacher and marry another. The sons inherit the wealth of their father; the daughters, however, obtain only a dowry. For a Brāhman who has remained true to his caste it is allowed to eat meat and to drink wine. On the Malabar coast they go about half-naked. They are the advisors of the kings and judges in religious disputes. All of them obey the highest master of their sect or caste, and if they act against their order, or its statutes, they are expelled from it, indeed exiled from the kingdom. The sacrificial priests and legal instructors among the

---

[37] [In Part II, chapter 6, 'Parvathi'.]

Brāhmans are maintained by the revenues of the temple where they are employed. Already in the division of the people into castes fields and lands are transferred to the best temples for the cultivation of rice in order to pay for the religious service and the maintenance of a certain number of priests from the income deriving from it. This institution exists even now in India in such kingdoms in which native-born kings who are dedicated to the national religious service rule. However, this relates really only to the sacrificial priests of a certain temple and the Samanaeans but not to those Brāhmans who are married.

KSHATRIYA

OF GOVERNMENT AND WARFARE

The second class of people in India consists of the royal caste that bears the name of kshatriya jāti.[38] Kshetram[39] means a woman, field, body, and temple. The kshatriyas indeed have no definite wife, if they do not wish to marry one; in peace time, they cultivate and work the fields; in war, they offer themselves for the service of the fatherland and live, besides, near temples. They are also called rājaputras, that is, sons of kings. The Indian kings must be born in this caste in order to attain the kingdom and government. However, at present, there are also some kings from the caste of brāhmans, as, for example, the King of Repelim[40] on the Malabar coast, who conducts sacrifices and also stands at the head of his state.

---

[38] [Caste; literally, 'by birth'.]

[39] [Paulinus errs in deriving kshatriya from kshetra, when the proper etymological base is kshatram, dominion. However, the term 'kshetrapati' (lord of the field) is sometimes used to designate a kshatriya.]

[40] [Edapalli (a district of Kochi), whose kings were originally brāhmans.]

TAB XXIXA – *Rāma Varma, King of Travancore, 1790 – after an Indian painting in the Museo Borgiano*

According to the most ancient Indian law, the king of a country is every time the first soldier in it and the official duties of these kshatriyas or rājaputras[41] are brought under the following heads:

> *Sandhi, peace:* The king must so far as possible seek to maintain peace and live in friendship with the neighbouring states.
>
> *Vigraham, killing:* If necessities make it a requirement, he must strive to kill in war the disturber of the peace.
>
> *Yānam, progress:* The king must be able to order the troops, inspect them, bring them

---

[41] People wrongly write Rajputs.

to the camp, lead them to the enemy, and have the ability not only to ride a horse or an elephant but also to lead these animals.

Āsanam, planning: The king must be able to set himself up in a suitable place and secure himself and his army.

Dvaidham: He must keep the troops in obedience and be able to prevent the devastation of the kingdom.

Āshrayam: He should strive to help the army as well as the nation and, in the case of wavering fortunes of war, be able to retreat skillfully into the fortifications.

Now these are the official duties of the kings, which they are obliged to fulfil and for which they therefore must possess prior knowledge and skill. The following, however, are the means that they must make use of for a good government:

Sāmam: They must be able to make themselves loved by the army and the people.

Dānam: They must be generous.

Bhedam: They must in a lawful way improve, train and punish.

Dandam: They should preside over and be useful to their state through industriousness and activity.

Rahasyam: They must possess secretiveness and not publicise any secrets.

Mandram: Before they undertake an important work, they are bound to confer and take precautionary measures.

Parikshanam: Before they involve the kingdom in a war, ample consideration of its consequences must come first.

Nyāyam: Kings must practise justice.

Kalpana: They must establish just and advantageous laws.

Nila: Finally, they themselves must act lawfully.

As supports and security for the kingdom the Indians list the following: first, for the regents:

Rājyam: This regent must really possess his kingdom.

Amātya: He must have a skillful minister.

Suharda: A faithful servant must stand at his side.

Cosham: He must have a treasury that is full and hidden.

Durggam: The king must be provided with sufficient defences.

Belam: He must have military force and an army.

These are the requirements of the kings and the kingdoms, which however differ from those of the military. For instance, after the soldiers are assembled, the military apparatuses procured, the army inspected, and the provisions distributed, the Indian troops were previously divided, not into legions, cohorts, squadrons, and ranks, but in the following orders and divisions:

> The first division was called Patti and in it were an elephant, a chariot, three riders, and five infantrymen.
>
> The second division, Senamukham, consisted of three elephants, as many chariots, nine riders, and fifteen infantrymen.
>
> The third division, Gutmam, contained nine elephants, nine chariots, twenty seven riders, and forty five infantrymen.
>
> The fourth division, Ganam, included twenty seven elephants, as many chariots, eighty seven riders, and hundred and thirty five infantrymen.
>
> The fifth division, Vāhini, consisted of eighty one elephants, as many chariots, two hundred and forty three riders, and four hundred and five infantrymen.
>
> The sixth division, Vrdana, included two hundred and forty three elephants, as many

chariots, seven hundred and twenty nine riders, and one thousand two hundred and fifteen infantrymen.

The seventh division, Chamu, contained seven hundred and twenty nine elephants, as many chariots, two thousand one hundred and eighty seven riders, and three thousand six hundred and forty four infantrymen.

The eight division, Anīkini, consisted of two thousand, one hundred and eighty seven elephants, a similar number of chariots, six thousand five hundred and sixty one riders, and ten thousand nine hundred and thirty five infantrymen.

The ninth division, or Akshohini, consisted of twenty one thousand eight hundred and seventy elephants, as many chariots, sixty five thousand six hundred and ten riders, hundred and nine thousand, three hundred and fifty infantrymen. This division concluded the entire army, if such an army was really present in India.

In this formation did the Indians in ancient times present their encounters, and apparently it was observed also by the army that fought under King Porus[42] against Alexander.[43] This explains how the Indian army on this occasion, regardless of its superior

---

[42] [Porus, or Purush, was a king of the Punjab who fought unsuccessfully against Alexander in the Battle of the Hydaspes (Jhelum river) in 326 B.C.]

[43] Curtius, Bk.8, ch.23.

force, was nevertheless defeated by the Macedonian. Later, the Indians followed first the Persian, then the Tartar,[44] and now the European order of battle. Tipu Sultan assumed the French war discipline, but the King of Travancore the English.

How easy it is, moreover, to call up an army in India is made clear from the following reasons.

Firstly, the second royal caste is at the same time the military caste and, since it has for its maintenance its allotted gardens and fields, it is constantly ready and prepared for war and it requires only a memorandum or signal to assemble it in a moment. Secondly, there is no need of any lengthy preparation, for the Indians fight mostly naked with bows and arrows, lances, shields, swords, pikes of different lengths, spades, javelins, and halberds. Shotguns are not used everywhere and not even introduced universally in any kingdom. Thirdly, the Indian soldier is very easy to maintain, for rice, fruits, vegetables, and rice-water were always and are still now his exclusive nourishment. He was similarly abstinent with regard to the use of opium and kanciava, or bhang,[45] leaves, the consumption of which is intoxicating; however, later the Arabs introduced this into India. The European soldier who indulges in intemperance and is addicted to arrack,[46] is, through his excesses, the heat, the poverty, the swamps, and the diseases that are caused by these, very easily exhausted and is no longer efficient after the first military campaign; so the English and Dutch prefer to pay Indian troops and prefer them to the European. Fourthly and lastly, in this way the Indian soldier returns, after the

---

[44] [Mogul.]

[45] [Cannabis.]

[46] [A drink made from sugarcane.]

end of the war, to his property and cultivates the fields that have been allotted to this caste from ancient times. This naturally reduces the pressure on the nation, promotes farming, and the country prospers thereby. But after the Tartars and the Europeans planted their method of waging war and their inhumane actions, mercenary soldiers have become common here too.

The kshatriyas were in the past clothed only in linen, wore sandals, and wound linen cloths around their head, as even today. They may wear the sacred thread the way the Brāhmans do, only they do not thereby obtain the right to explain the laws but merely to listen to the explications of these. The kings received their education from the philosophers and that in houses that lay close to the temples, and this custom is still found in Tibet and on the Malabar coast. For, there, the young Tesho Lama[47] in the Lhasa cloister and, here, the Cochin and Travancore kings are taught in buildings close to temples.

This royal caste has been dissolved in many parts of India and in its place the third caste, that of the Shūdras and Nairs,[48] has entered that provides military service. Neither the one nor the other of these castes is bound to a real and legitimate marriage but among them everything depends on discretion and inclination; therefore the man can discard the wife whom he has once taken and a courtesan can arbitrarily leave a lover whom she has received. This is the reason why the courtesan receives visits from men of this caste in her house but is only rarely introduced into the man's house. The right to visit her depends solely on her permission and the conditions that she

---

[47] [The European name for the Panchen (Scholar) Lama.]

[48] [A ruling caste of Kerala that is marked by matrilineal customs.]

thereby makes to her lover. Meanwhile, a courtesan receives, according to an ancient custom, on the first visit, a garment of his linen. If she accepts it, this is a sign that she agrees with the desires of the man and grants him intercourse with her, indeed a right to her, as it were, and this intercourse has then, in a certain way, a legal respectability.

This undefined affair, this freedom to bind oneself to a courtesan, and soon to separate, this choice determined by the place and circumstances, left to mutual arbitrariness, and the indifference of the father that follows therefrom in relation to his children, whom he does not in the meantime know even by their appearance, all of this, I say, could almost certainly make one think that this caste must finally die out and be dissolved; but the unchanging nature, the great age and the long duration of this custom prove the opposite. For, this caste still exists, and will apparently also last as long as the Indian religion and the original institutions of this nation are respected.[49]

---

[49] [I may reproduce here Forster's note: 'The author seems to contradict himself to a certain extent in that he previously stated that this caste is indeed already dissolved in many places in India. Nevertheless, I think that his second opinion is well-founded. If the courtesans were of another caste than the royal then of course even their sons would not belong to the latter and it would be a wonder that they have been able to maintain themselves up to now. But since the courtesans may not be of any other caste than the royal, as the author explains directly afterwards, their sons remain in the same and the entire difference consists in the fact that they do not obtain the inheritance of their fathers but of their uncles and, in these circumstances, only an unusual sterility could devastate this caste. I may be wrong but I consider the institution of this caste as extraordinarily shrewd politically. For the soldier here has his land for which he fights through self-interest but no family of his own that he might fall into the danger of relaxing idly with it instead of confronting the enemy. If the actual results do not correspond in

NĀLEVARNAM

The sons produced from such a union enter fully into the camp of their mothers. They remain – as demanded by traditional custom and right – with the courtesan, are brought up in the house of their mother and inherit the wealth of their uncle without taking any consideration of the father; rather, his sister, if he has one, must likewise nourish and educate the sons born of her, whereafter they then equally inherit from their uncle.

It is considered a crime of the courtesans if they have to do with a man of another caste and, if the latter is of a lower caste, they are, if they are found guilty of their crime, usually sold out as slaves. The sons of kings, therefore, do not enter as heirs into the estate of their father but only the first-born son of the sister of the king inherits from his uncle and usually bears the title of second king, just as his mother, or the sister of his uncle, bears the title of queen. That hereby no consideration is taken of the actual sons of the king and their mother has already been indicated. The latter indeed have legal claims to a certain living but not to any special status. In this way does it occur even today with the sons of king Perumpadapil[50] and those of Rāma Varman.[51]

As the reason of this law and this custom the Indians point out that thereby the royal and warrior blood is maintained unmixed, that the properties are not transferred by the women from one family to another, that the men, freed of the care of children and wives, would be more vigorous in war and that, finally,

---

modern times to this secure presupposition, the causes of this lie clearly in other circumstances.']

[50] [The kings of Cochin were called Perampadapu Veliya Thampuran (the great lord of Perampadapu).]

[51] [Rāma Varman (1724-1798) was king of Travancore from 1758.]

the women are freed of the danger of falling, in the case of a long absence of their husbands, into certain incontinence, and the men would have as little to fear of having to nourish sons foisted on them.

VAISHYA

OF FARMING

The third noble caste bears the name Vaishya jāti. The following are considered their occupations:

Farming,
Animal husbandry,
Trade, or the sale of agricultural products.

Sri Rāma, or the youthful Bacchus,[52] was supposed to

---

[52] [Paulinus relies here on Arrian's Indica, VII, which relates that '(Megasthenes) tells us further that the Indians were in old times nomadic, like those Skythians who did not till the soil, hut roamed about in their wagons, as the seasons varied, from one part of Skythia to another, neither dwelling in towns nor worshipping in temples; and that the Indians likewise had neither towns nor temples of the gods, but were so barbarous that they wore the skins of such wild animals as they could kill, and subsisted on the bark of trees; that these trees were called in Indian speech tāla, and that there grew on them, as there grows at the tops of the palm-trees, a fruit resembling balls of wool; that they subsisted also on such wild animals as they could catch, eating the flesh raw, – before, at least, the coming of Dionysos into India. Dionysos, however, when he came and had conquered the people, founded cities and gave laws to these cities, and introduced the use of wine among the Indians, as he had done among the Greeks, and taught them to sow the land, himself supplying ,seeds for the purpose, – either because Triptolemos, when he was sent by Demeter to sow all the earth, did

NĀLEVARNAM

have first taught Indians farming and for that reason he is also called Siravānni, that is, the ploughman. To him is also attributed the unification of the Indians living scattered until then and their progress from pastoral to urban life. But this opinion soon appears in its illogicality when one considers that farming and pastoralism are assigned to the same caste, and thus depends on the Indian legal and civil system. Consequently, the establishment of those two activities can be traced back to no other than King Manu,[53] to whom is attributed the division of the Indian people

---

not reach these parts, or this must have been some Dionysos who came to India before Triptolemos, and gave the people the seeds of cultivated plants. It is also said that Dionysos first yoked oxen to the plough, and made many of the Indians husbandmen instead of nomads, and furnished them with the implements of agriculture; and that the Indians worship the other gods, and Dionysos himself in particular, with cymbals and drums (compare Diodorus Siculus' account above p.15), because he so taught them; and that he also taught them the Satyric dance, or, as the Greeks call it, the Kordax; and that he instructed the Indians to let their hair grow long in honour of the god, and to wear the turban; and that he taught them to anoint themselves with unguents, so that even up to the time of Alexander the Indians were marshalled for battle to the sound of cymbals and drums.'

Rāma is an incarnation of Vishnu rather than of Shiva (or his son Skanda/Muruga), who is normally identified with Dionysus. However, Balarāma, the eighth incarnation of Vishnu after Rāma (and brother of Krishna), is also called Halāyudha, meaning 'The one who uses the plough as his weapon' and is associated with agriculture as well as with the consumption of palm-wine (from the palm, tāla, mentioned by Megasthenes). Indeed, the Brahmānda Purāna states that Rudra-Shiva himself was called Halāyudha (see A. Parpola, 'Bala-Rāma and Sītā: On the origins of the Rāmāyana', Indologica Taurinensia, Vol.30-21, 2004).]

[53] [In the *Bhāgavata Purāna*, VIII,24, the survivor of the "flood", Manu (the counterpart of Noah) is called Satyavrata, King of Dravida.]

into castes. But, since Sri Rāma represents the diurnal sun and the entire foundation of Indian religion, as well as many customs and traditions in fashion in this country, is to be derived not at all from the artificial and scholarly observation of the stars but indeed from the merely natural and simple glance at the heavens, can it indeed be inferred with probability that such early and necessary skills as those that pastoral life and farming demand should have been separated from astronomy? that they should have had another inventor than necessity? and, finally, that one of these skills is older than the other? Thus, however, the natural, simple, and correct establishment of legislation – even at the time of the first urban establishment among men – demanded that, where priests were appointed for the accomplishment of the honouring of the gods, and kings as the leaders of the people, even farmers, shepherds and such people as brought the produced goods into circulation were present. This admirable arrangement innate in human nature most clearly demonstrates the original unity of this people and the hoary age of this legislation. Farmers must hand over wheat, rice, milk, and butter to those who do not occupy themselves with the production of food and, while the priests provide the religious service and the kings worry about peace or conduct wars, a third caste must cultivate the fields and provide to the former the necessary food.

As respected and revered as the first and second caste are in India so much too is this third since it stands in closest relationship with them and is utterly indispensable and does not practise any dishonest business and constitutes the foundation of the entire state. Here there does not enter at all any thought of trade that promotes luxury among these and weakens the strength of the empire but the legislation is characterized even here by its simplicity in that it restricts the lifestyle, work, and occupation of this third noble caste to farming, animal husbandry and to trade with the products gained from these. In this way, these laws have existed already for more than three thousand years and should, therefore not be criticized so often in Europe.

The Indian temples as well as the Christian churches and the lands lent to them are freed from all assessments or taxes,[54] and the churches of the St.

---

[54] The pagan King of Cochin bestowed on the Catholic priests the date palm grove and city of Verapolis. Here is a letter of grant composed on a copper plate in the vernacular Malabārian language:

'Greetings from the King to the priests of Verapolis! We herewith free the date palm grove Tāttārachery up to now possessed by us and lying in the district of Verapolis, and the Christian church there, from all duties and taxes, assessments or other impositions that both we and our heirs, successors or ministers have placed or will place in future and gift to you that land from the surface of the earth to the bottom of the water, and bestow it too, wherefore we have had this instrument or letter of gift, exemption and insurance composed. The boundaries of this date palm grove is marked in the morning by the river flowing there, in the afternoon by the Mundenchery date palm grove, whose northern limit it touches, in the evening the Mārāba date palm grove, whose eastern side it touches, and at midnight the Maniyandra date palm grove with its southern side. Now what is enclosed within these four boundaries, all of that, up to the bottom of the water, we grant, gift and bestow upon you as your property and possession and, in order that none of our heirs or anybody else may make a claim on it, demand or collect duties, levies or taxes, we free this property of yours from all such burdens so that you may establish your religious practices unhindered and that date palm grove as well as all that it contains may serve you as you will for it is your possession, which we have granted to you, confirm it granted and relinquish it to your possession. This order I, Rāman, have composed by my own hand, agreeing in everything with the words of the king in Kerekal

Thomas Christians,[55] called Nasrāni, in Malabar have enjoyed this privilege already since the time of King Cheraman Perumal,[56] that is, almost from the sixth century. It is an ancient, general, and unchangeable principle of the Indians that nothing that belongs to Īshvara, or the highest god, or is sacred to him, must be touched.

The schools, or academies, in which the young Brāhmans are educated and receive instruction in Sanskrit, in the liturgy and the religious ritual, in astronomy and other sciences, which are all included in the general name of Shāstram, also have their own lands and revenues that are similarly freed of any state taxes. The collection of these revenues is transferred to a Brāhman who bears, from this function, the title Snātaka and undertakes the payment of requirements to the teachers as well as to the entire institution, which is called yogam. This institution exists even at present in the academy in Trichur in Malabar, where the form of the ancient Indian religion under its dedicated kings has been preserved unchanged, whereas in the northern regions the original constitution and religion, as well as the ancient customs and rights, have been mixed with others and changed in their form through the Tartars,

---

Palace in the year 860 of Kollam, in the month of Virgo.

860 in Kollam is our 1673, and the month of Virgo is our September. The civil time calculation of the Malabārians thus begins, as we see, with the building of the city of Kollam. See *Alph. Malabar*, p.21.

[55] [The St. Thomas Christians are a Christian community in Kerala who are called Nasrani (Nazarenes) and trace their origins to the arrival of St. Thomas in India in the first century. They were first organized ecclesiastically under the 'Province of India' by Timothy I (780-823), Patriarch of the Church of the East.]

[56] [Cheraman Perumal is the Chera dynasty that established the earliest kingdoms in Kerala.]

NĀLEVARNAM

Arabs and English. Since India has been subjected to so many rulers whose first care was to eradicate the ancient laws and set new ones in their place, it would generally be difficult to represent the feudal system, the customs, and ancient institutions of this country, with a definite coherence. This is also connected to the depredation of India and the frightful devastation of this glorious country through angaris,[57] assessments, taxes, etc. How often does one have the opportunity in India to wonder at the greed for gold of the Europeans, the satisfaction of which makes even the most violent means acceptable to them, and how skillful was the reply of the King of Travancore, which he gave to an European when the latter complained to him of the strictness of the levy of a tax, saying: 'You yourselves have taught me strictness and violence in government.'

On the Malabar coast, out of ten measures of grain, which yield hundred measures of rice in the production, as many as thirty measures of this must be paid to the king. This tenth is called muppara, and it is decreed by an ancient law, to which are subjected the Vaishyas, Shūdras, Nairs, the St. Thomas Christians, the Arabs born in India – who bear the name of Māpulas – and finally all those that have received fields from the king and cultivate them. Nobody other than the temples, churches, academies, and cloisters of the samanas[58] receives a property of a field or grove of

---

[57] ['The angaris are an ancient institution of oriental despotism and consist indeed in certain post stations with allotted horses for the couriers who are free, if they are lacking in horses, to take them where they may find them, indeed even from a travelling rider who happens to meet them. Then the owner must then run to the next station in order to get his horse back or to show the way to it (see Chardin, *Voyage en Perse*, Vol. II, p.242).' – Note of Forster.]

[58] [Shramanas, see above.]

date palms; indeed, according to an ancient traditional custom, the lower castes of the nation cannot have any landed property because otherwise, it would have to be feared that they would not only leave their present situation and their profession, but that they might also, through merit, property, ambition, sexual strictness and refinement, be mixed with the other castes and in this way the legal system of India might be damaged.

The field is ploughed with a wooden plough, not with an iron ploughshare since the soil is light in most places of this country. The harrow is not used at all and as little does one make use of a weeding instrument, for rice grows in low and moist fields and weeds are pulled out by hand. In many places in India the field is sown twice and harvested twice too. If the tracts of land are unfruitful, one digs in their midst, and at certain distances, holes that are filled with cut branches and leaves and, when they decay, are used as excellent manure which fertilizes the field in such a way that it is not necessary to leave it fallow. When rains are lacking they scoop in a bucket or vessel that is tied to a pole water from the lakes, rivers and ponds and conduct it through canals and channels to their fields, as Sonnerat[59] has described more extensively. One would be seriously mistaken if one judged – and therefore wished to criticize – the manner and method of Indian farming in general according to the procedure of the people on the Coromandel coast.[60] From Bengal and the Malabar coast an amount of rice is transferred for the sustenance

---

[59] See Sonnerat, *op.cit.*, Vol.I, p.189 of the octavo edition. [Pierre Sonnerat (1748-1814) was a French naturalist whose Voyage aux Indes orientales et à Chine, 1782, contained accounts of the religion, customs and crafts of South India.]

[60] [The Coromandel (from Chola Mandalam, the Chola land) is the southeastern coast of India.]

of the Indians on the Coromandel coast, so one must derive the knowledge of Indian farming from the former and not the latter, where the ground is parched and unproductive and the people are devoted more to trade or weaving and dying their cloths than with agriculture.

According to certain statements that are found in Arrian, Strabo and Curtius[61] one must think that the Brāhmans, already in most ancient times, on account of farming, prepared journals or calendars. It seemed to them, following Nature and astronomy, to divide the year – according to the movement of the sun (for they always maintain that the sun moves around the earth)[62] and according to the twelve constellations through which the sun moves as it were – into as many months,[63] and this division exists even at present in India.

No less did astronomy demand the observation of the course and influence, the connection and effect, of the sun, moon, and other planets, to note what connection there exists between the latter and the earth and especially farming and, following that, to determine the sowing and harvesting times, to designate the good and bad days or record them with an iron stylus on palm leaves, to predict rain or pleasant weather from the movement of the wind and the stars and, finally, to attribute a special power to the stars, which they consider to be intelligences and worship as divinities.

---

[61] [Quintus Curtius Rufus, *Historiae Alexandri Magni Macedonis.*]

[62] It does not appear that it can be taken as certain that the ancient Brāhmans had placed the earth in the middle of the universe, indeed some think that the Indian philosopher Yavanācharya taught attraction and placed the sun in the middle of the universe (see *Asiatic Researches*, p.430).

[63] See Waltheri, *Doctrina indica de tempore*, p.153, appendix to Bayeri, *Historia regni bactriani* and the latter's *Chronologia scytica vetus*, in the *Comentariis academ.*, St. Petersburg, Vol.III, p.302.

That the Brāhmans occupied themselves already in antiquity with astronomy and ascribed to the planets diverse powers, even a certain influence on the earth, is illustrated only too clearly from the ancient names of these. Shani is the name of Saturn, and its meaning is moist, cold. It is also called Shaneshvara, or the Lord of Moisture, Gauri, the one born on or from the Ganges, Mandā, the slow one, on account of the large circle that it has to make around the sun and which it travels therefore only in a long period of time, Pangu, the limping one, indeed finally it is also called simply Time or the planet that requires a very long time for its revolution. Saturn, therefore, is allegorically called Chronos or Time and is depicted as an old man and sometimes holds a sickle in his hand because he is a symbol of Time because the accomplishment of its revolution is possible only in a long duration. He also bears a serpent as a symbol of life because he, like the other planets, possesses equally the characteristic of vivification and has an influence on earthly things. The Malabārans and Tamils consider him to be a Tabassa, that is, a being with insight because he, like Budha or Mercury,[64] looks upon the divinity of the sun and revolves around it. Budha, or Dharma, is the advisor of Saturn because he is next to the sun, the highest Indian god and so he is called also the All-knowing, Understanding and Insight. He shows to Saturn who is farther from him the path for the completion of its revolution around the sun and for this reason too he is considered the messenger of the gods, the leader of wanderers, and the scribe of Saturn.

---

[64] [The Romans identified Wotan with Mercury, see Tacitus, *Germania*, 9.]

NĀLEVARNAM

TAB XXX - Shani - after an Indian painting in the Museo Borgiano

The moon, further, bears the names of coolness, moisture, brown, bent backwards, the Lord; the planet of great size is called Jupiter, the Insightful and teacher, and Venus Vshaena, the always fecund star, or the morning star. This seems to prove that the ancient Brāhmans were very knowledgeable in astronomy and that this science, along with its astronomical fables and eastern allegories, was transferred from them to Greece and Latium.

The age of these intelligences or planets is very different from the age of men and the heavenly calculation of time greatly exceeds that of the human race. The Indians calculate the age of their nation from that age and that it, therefore, rises very high is self-evident. One day of the heavenly intelligences and gods makes one of our years; one year passed by them has the length of three hundred and sixty five of our years, and four heavenly ages are constituted of twelve thousand years of the heavenly intelligences. The Indians now establish their calculation of time according to this calculation and establish their fabulous age.

SHŪDRA

OF THE MECHANICAL ARTS

The fourth noble caste in India is that of the artists and handicraftsmen which contributes no less than the other three to the maintenance of the kingdom and was, therefore, at the time this political institution was created, honoured with nobility. To this caste belong goldsmiths, metal casters, smiths, carpenters, garland makers, painters, doctors, tailors, fortune-tellers, magicians, cloth weavers, and many other workers.

But not noble and marked by a certain infamy are the two castes of Pariahs and Puleyas. The first of these castes has to do with cadavers that have fallen into the water or also naturally dead animals. The people of this caste skin cows, remove the skins of other animals, and eat meat. From these occupations of theirs they receive the names Chandāla[65] and Nishāda[66] that designate low men who must be shunned.

---

[65] [Chandālas are untouchable since, as hunters, fishermen, and butchers, they deal with dead animals.]

[66] [Nishādas are aboriginal Indian hunters and fishermen.]

The other non-noble caste of the Puleyas consists of slaves and, in ancient times, was, legally and traditionally, formed of such people who, on account of an offence against the decrees and their caste, were driven out of it, forfeited their nobility, and made slaves. Now, since these men propagate their type through courtesans, who have had a similar fate owing to a similar crime, there arose from this process this caste which exists up to the present day and will apparently exist so long as the present legal institution of India exists. From the reason of the formation of this caste has arisen the present customary phrase 'puleyādunu,' which means to be driven out of one's caste, become contaminated, or bring infamy upon oneself, whether this happens through association with a courtesan from another caste or otherwise, through some other improper and shameful action. But I return to the Shūdra caste.

TAB XXXII – *Puleya – after an Indian painting in the Museo Borgiano*

All handicraftsmen have their chiefs, who are called Kulashreshtas. The liberal, as well as the mechanical, arts bear the common name Shilpashāstram. Those who are occupied in it are divided into several guilds for the maintenance of the public peace and order, and all stand under the guild masters, who are normally the judges of their guilds. All trials that concern the guild – no matter how they are called – are brought before it, examined in an assembly of the elders, according to the ancient custom, and decided upon according to tradition, and the judgement, if the case is difficult, drawn up according to the majority of votes. The office and duty of these guild chiefs, therefore, binds them to nip in the bud discord and hatred in the families, to prevent rising unrest, to maintain the rights of their guild, to rule on disputed goods, to endow poor girls from the guild treasury, receive notices of marriages, make divorces available when the spouses cannot live with each other, or, on account of an offence of one of them, ask to be separated, to warn criminals and, if they do not wish to improve, to go to the king and request him to expel them out of the caste using his power and to sell them in the fatherland or abroad as slaves for a payment that flows into the royal treasury. These rights of the guild chiefs are valid even today on the Malabar coast although they have been much reduced since the time that mercenary soldiers began to be employed in the place of the old patrician warriors and foreigners began to be recruited. The latter indeed extended more than a little the power of the kings and the ministers stopped deferring to the judgement of the guild chiefs and imposed arbitrary rewards or punishments of private persons.

Woodcarvers, sculptors, and brassfounders were known in India from time immemorial, as the most ancient temples indeed prove.[67] As regards the depiction of human figures and especially the making of large statues, the Indians indeed lack the liveliness and correct style that we admire in similar artworks of the Greeks and Romans but in the depiction of smaller figures, in the representation of wars, triumphal chariots, and in the adornment of temple façades, there is a skill, a beautiful and pleasing simplicity and, finally, such an elegant diversity such as we do not observe in the ancient Egyptian monuments. That the large statues lack art and correctness does not lie in the clumsiness of the Indian genius and a weakness of judgement of this people but in the demands of the priests and sects who base themselves on opinions and mysteries and for whom it is sufficient to see the concept of a divinity brought according to the secrets of the religious representation of the same to a depiction that is for this reason inharmonious and incorrect. Thus there is, for example, nothing more formless than the statue and depiction of the goddess Lakshmi, who is normally represented seated and with crooked, crossed, and repugnant feet. But that does not happen without a mysterious reason, for Lakshmi is the Earth, which gives birth and by giving birth nourishes and vivifies, and is therefore depicted as the great Mother in a child-bearing position, as it were. For this reason did an Indian artist who had to mould certain pictures of gods in bronze and who was criticized for their misshapen appearance reply that he could not deviate from the prescribed form in order not to be considered

---

[67] I refer here to the temples in Ellora, Salcette, Rameshvaram and that on the island of Elephanta. That Alexander built these cannot at all be proven; rathermore their entire construction and decoration as well as the certain deduction from historical statements speak for native builders.

a frivolous scorner of the law and custom, accused of error by the priests, and set before the chief of his guild in a bad light. This is also the reason why it is forbidden to all painters, sculptors, and founders to sell a painting or a statue before these are inspected by priests, found to be good, consecrated with holy water, and accepted into the register of idols.

As regards medicine, it is also, as Strabo[68] already noted a long time ago, practiced by the Indians but since they view the transmigration of souls as an article of belief it cannot of course but be that they abjure every form of healing that necessitates a blood-letting. But, as false as that doctrine may be, it still contributes – since it is suited to the mild climate and the character of the people – not a little to the morality of the Indians. Therefrom arises their gentle temperament, their friendly treatment of men as well as animals, indeed I would say their love of these, which they stretch to the point of superstition; thence the few murders among the pagan natives of this country, their compassion for the miserable and their benevolence even in the punishment of crimes. But even for that reason they exclude the opening of veins from their remedies or make use of it only in the greatest emergency. As little do they know of, or use, the Caesarean section or enemas, and illnesses that they can heal without these methods, through the simple or collected use of herbal remedies, they either reject entirely or try to stop with common or superstitious methods. This cannot be surprising for, just as the Indians do not feel any strong emotions, they are attended by the defect of a certain physical sluggishness and weakness. They are extremely superstitious, patient to a defect, depend excessively

---

[68] Bk. XV.

on their gods, look to receive oracles from them, are defective in the use of medical remedies, tolerate their sufferings very submissively if they think that they observe that medicine does not improve anything and that the gods are not fair to them and give themselves without fear to Īshvara, or the god of vengeance. One sees very many of them lying on the sickbed with a submissiveness that can lead one to conclude a total lack of intellect and sense, and – no matter how much their physical forces have already been decimated by their suffering – many die peacefully, without their face betraying any sign of death.

As little as the knowledge is that the Indians have of medicine and surgery there are still hardly any illnesses – those general national weaknesses excepted – that the Brāhmans are not able to cure. And there is also in this country a large amount of medical writings, and boys learn from the most tender childhood on about the herbs and their qualities so that one sees ten-year olds of their race that one is forced to wonder at as experienced herbalists. The analysis of plants and the description of their powers is, according to the standards of ancient and modern experiments and long usage, in those writings as perfect and precise as possible.[69]

That the Indians practised the art of writing already in very ancient times is confirmed by Strabo,[70] and the materials on which they write may well have followed

---

[69] One who has acquired knowledge of the language can find much information about this topic in the numerous manuscripts of the present Bibliotheque nationale in Paris, especially in the book of the Atharveda to be found there equally which deals with the fourth law of the Indians or the functions of the fourth caste. See also Sonnerat, *op.cit.*, Vol.I, ch.5, p.74, and ch.9, p.174. *Asiatic Researches*, Vol.I, p.408 and p.428, and Niebuhr, *op.cit.*, Vol.II, p.17.

[70] *op.cit.*

one by one the order that Pliny states.[71] At first the Indians may have been encouraged to write on the dry and easily available palm leaves, and therefore, the number of books written on such inscribed leaves which are called Grantha when they are tied together by a thread drawn through two holes on both joints of the leaves and two tables likewise containing palm leaves. From these books has Sanskrit improperly obtained the same name Grantham, since the language and the script in which such ancient books are composed is indeed Sanskrit.

TAB XXXI – *An Indian scribe – after an Indian painting in the Museo Borgiano*

---

[71] *Historia naturalis*, Bk.13, ch.11.

After the books of palm leaves perhaps paper books came into use, especially in North India, where palms are less common. How ancient the weaving of fine linen among this people is is revealed by the *Periplus* of Arrian. From cotton, which served for the manufacture of that linen, they then prepared also a sort of rather raw paper platters which, when their surfaces were rubbed and smoothed, were thereafter tacked together into books in diverse ways. When the King of Travancore writes to respectable men not under his rule he makes use of a European type of paper, folds the letter, and covers it with his seal; on the other hand, if writes to his subjects, this happens on palm-leaves. As a sample of the way in which such letters are composed may follow here a letter from the said king to the bishop and mission priests at Verapolis[72] in 1787:

Letter

for the perusal of the Bishop and the fathers at Verapolis

I have read your letter sent to me and learnt the entire process from it. At the same time you have now conveyed to me the outcome of the process. I hope that no obstacle to the convention of your (Christian) law will be placed without cause. If, however, such a thing should occur, I shall consult with you and mediate the matter. I, the chief secretary Pira

---

[72] As evidence of this sort of books are to be considered the Tibetan, Peguanian, Indian and Chinese paper manuscripts and the diploma written on silk cloth of the great Lama of Tibet in the library of the *Congregatio de propaganda fide*. (Verapolis is the present-day Varappuzha, a suburb of the city of Kochi.)

Ciudum Perumal Mahādevan, have therefore composed this letter following the command of his majesty

Shri Padmanābhan

(the king's own signature)

On the outside is found the inscription:

> Reply of the king to the bishop and the fathers at Verapolis.

At the same time as the use of paper books there appears the use of copper plates since laws, privileges and other important documents could not be entrusted with certainty to palm-leaves and cotton paper. The English have discovered many such copper plates in Calcutta,[73] the first of which contains a land grant and, no matter how one calculates Indian eras, is to be dated to the period before the first century A.D. But hereby it is to be noted[74] that the Northern Indians count the years not merely according to the era of Shālivāhana,[75] of whom we spoke earlier, but also, and indeed commonly, according to the era of Vikramāditya.[76] The

---

[73] *Asiatic Researches*, pp.123, 131, 279, 357.

[74] Which Niebuhr, *op.cit.*, Vol.II, p.27, has also noted.

[75] [Shālivāhana is a legendary Indian king, who is supposed to have established the Shālivāhana (or Shāka) era in the Julian year 78 when he defeated several foreign invaders including the Shakas (Scythians).]

[76] [Vikramāditya is a legendary king of India who is also credited with the defeat of the Shakas and the establishment of the Vikrama Samvat era beginning in 57 B.C. He is in some Hindu texts described

year 1848 of this era is our 1791; if therefore it is apparent that it says in that copper plate that: King Devapāla or Gopāla[77] made that land-grant in the thirty third year of the era of King Vikramāditya, one cannot, without difficulty, date the issuing of this document other than to 22 B.C.[78] In this document reference is made to Sugueda, that is, Buddha, and further to the goddess Lakshmi, to Rāma, Lakshmana, and the sects and castes mentioned up to now. Thus the Indians do not lack their own documents and, according to these as well as to their books, it can be maintained with conviction that the use of Sanskrit in writing is very ancient and that everything that has been quoted up to now by me, especially from the statements of Amarasimha's book,[79] is valid unchangeably still today.

The Indians write with an iron stylus with admirable skill on palm leaves and that while they are standing,

---

as the grandfather of Shālivāhana.]

[77] These names are incorrectly written in the *Asiatic Researches* as Debpāl and Gopāl.

[78] Some, following the tradition of the Indians, consider Vikramāditya as the father of King Sālivagana or Salbahan, as, for instance, Niebuhr, op.cit., where he, like Wilford and Wilkins in the Asiatic Researches, writes both names wrongly. Some also write Vicramāditya and that corresponds very much to the pure and original Sanskrit. Vikram or Vicram means the Extraordinary, but Āditya means the sun and so that full name means the extraordinary, the greatest sun. However, whoever this king may have been, it is sufficient that from his death onwards a special historical era begins that cannot be doubted since it is mentioned in the Indian documents. It is found especially in all the copper plates of that sort that have been known up to now in India. Thus one has to mark this era next to that of King Sālivagana. It is indeed wrong when some maintain that that first calculation of time begins in 250 A.D.

[79] [Amarasimha (4th c.) was a Sanskrit grammarian who compiled a famous lexicon called *Amarkosha*.]

seated, walking about or lying down, indeed often without having anything to support themselves on. The number of scribes is great and as great the number of manuscripts that one can read only after great effort.

I end these investigations here with an Indian saying or shloka:[80]

> Love the company of honest and worthy people, hope that the other person fares well and do good yourself; honour your teacher and master, study the sciences, adhere to your wife alone, flee and shun the sins of the world, be devoted to your creator, curtail your passions, avoid the company of bad people. Praise and respect will be bestowed upon the man who acts thus!

---

[80] Already Diogenes Laertes, *De vitis philosophorum in proemium*, Rome edition, p.2, says: 'They say that the gymnosophists philosophized in riddles and short axioms that mainly concluded that one should worship the gods, do nothing evil, and be virtuous.' This sort of philosophizing exists even today in India and such short aphorisms are called shlokams. The number of these in India is great and boys learn them by-heart from earliest childhood on. Apothegms too are not lacking through which the Indians seek to form the morals of their youth.

OTHER BOOKS BY ALEXANDER JACOB

THE GRAIL – TWO STUDIES

A proper understanding of the significance of the cultic object called the Holy Grail has eluded most scholars who have confined their research to western European literary and cultural sources, especially since the originally Celtic story of the Holy Grail underwent numerous bewildering metamorphoses in the romances of the Middle Ages.

It was the Indologist Leopold von Schroeder's reading of the Grail story (1910) in the light of his knowledge of Indic mythology that first achieved a dramatic expansion of the field of Holy Grail scholarship. The only other scholar who developed a comprehensive comparative mythological study of the

Grail was perhaps Julius Evola in his Il *Mistero del Graal e la Tradizione Ghibellina dell'Impero* (1937).

Schroeder's fascinating elucidation of some of the key symbols of the Grail legends using his knowledge of ancient Indian literature is amplified by Alexander Jacob's reconstruction of the cosmological basis of these symbols and his analysis of the solar rituals that characterized the diverse yet related religions of the ancient Indo-Europeans.

INDO-EUROPEAN MYTHOLOGY AND RELIGION: ESSAYS

The essays presented in this collection are based on Alexander Jacob's earlier works, *Ātman: A Reconstruction of the Solar Cosmology of the Indo-Europeans*, Hildesheim: Georg Olms, 2005 and *Brahman: A Study of the Solar Rituals of the Indo-Europeans*, Hildesheim: Georg Olms, 2012. They expand on the cosmological and religious themes discussed in these books with special reference to the origins and development of the Indic and European spiritual traditions. Those familiar with the earlier works will not be surprised that Dr. Jacob's view of the term 'Indo-European' is rather more comprehensive than the more restricted term 'Āryan' that has hitherto been widely used as a synonym of it. And those interested in the Āryan ethos itself – chiefly on account of the German use of the term during the last war – may be surprised to learn that it does not consist in nationalistic virtues so much as in spiritual discipline and development – and that this development is characteristic of the religions of very extended and diversified branches of the Indo-European family.

VEDANTA, PLATO, AND KANT
BY PAUL DEUSSEN
TRANSLATED BY ALEXANDER JACOB

"The Kantian worldview, which always underlay all religion, philosophy, and art, could not have been the eternal truth if it did not emerge more or less clearly everywhere that the human mind penetrated into the depths, as this occurred, for example, in India through the Upanishads of the Vedas and the Vedanta based on them and in Greece through Parmenides and Plato. To consider both these phenomena in the light of the Kantian philosophy is the task that we have set ourselves here." - *Paul Deussen*

Vedanta, Plato, and Kant is a new translation. The book presents a defense of Shankara's Advaita Vedānta philosophy as well as an elucidation of the Greek Idealistic doctrines of Parmenides and Plato. In all these schools of thought, Deussen detects a similar basic understanding of the world as a mere appearance distinct from Ideal Reality. He approximated this understanding to the Kantian notion of 'things in themselves' (Dinge-an-sich) and noted a degeneration of the original Vedic and Upanishadic worldview in the philosophies that followed, such as the Sāmkhya and Buddhism, just as there was a corruption of Parmenides' doctrine of Being in the philosophy of his pupil Zeno. Similarly, he believes that Kant's revolutionary Idealistic insights in Germany were also distorted by the post-Kantian thinkers and not generally understood in their original form except by Arthur Schopenhauer (1788-1860), who developed the doctrine of the world as a mere representation produced by the innate intuitive forms within the Intellect – Space, Time, and Causality.

Includes a preface by Alexander Jacob (Translator).

AGNI-VĀYU-ĀDITYA:
THE INDO-EUROPEAN TRINITY OF FIRE

This abrégé of Jacob's 2005 study *Ātman: A Reconstruction of the Solar Cosmology of the Indo-Europeans* (Hildesheim: Georg Olms) focuses on the cosmological insights that inform ancient Indo-European religions and, in particular, on the most significant trinity worshipped by the ancient Indo-Āryans – Agni-Vāyu-Āditya – which represents the forms that the cosmic fire takes in the underworld of Earth before it is installed as the sun in the Heaven of our universe. This is not a sociological Trinity, as Dumézil's studies, for example, would lead one to believe. Rather, it is an understanding of the divine fire that informs the macrocosm as well as the human microcosm.

The present essay should thus serve to correct the misleading sociological orientations of Dumézilian comparative mythology. At the same time, it will give the reader a glimpse into the extraordinary depth of vision of the prisca theologia of the Indo-Europeans.

www.ingramcontent.com/pod-product-compliance
Lightning Source LLC
Chambersburg PA
CBHW051711040426
42446CB00008B/819